Contemporary Wedding & Love Songs

ISBN 0-7935-8063-3

7777 W. BLUEMOUND RD. P.O. BOX 13819 MILWAUKEE, WI 53213

For all works contained herein:
Unauthorized copying, arranging, adapting, recording or public performance is an infringement of copyright.
Infringers are liable under the law.

Visit Hal Leonard Online at
www.halleonard.com

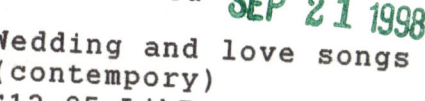

Contemporary Wedding & Love Songs

4	All I Ask of You *Barbra Streisand*	63	If We Fall in Love Tonight *Rod Stewart*
9	Always *Bon Jovi*	68	Love of a Lifetime *Firehouse*
18	Beautiful in My Eyes *Joshua Kadison*	75	Love Remains *Collin Raye*
22	Can You Feel the Love Tonight *Elton John*	80	Save the Best for Last *Vanessa Williams*
26	Don't Know Much *Linda Ronstadt and Aaron Neville*	86	Valentine *Jim Brickman*
32	Endless Love *Luther Vandross and Mariah Carey*	90	The Wedding Song *Kenny G*
37	Grow Old with Me *Mary Chapin Carpenter*	92	When You Say Nothing at All *Alison Krauss & Union Station*
40	Have I Told You Lately *Rod Stewart*	97	A Whole New World *Peabo Bryson and Regina Belle*
52	I Believe in You and Me *Whitney Houston*	106	You and I *Eddie Rabbitt and Crystal Gayle*
45	I Finally Found Someone *Barbra Streisand and Bryan Adams*	110	You Must Love Me *Madonna*
58	I'll Still Be Loving You *Restless Heart*		

Pomeroy Public Library

All I Ask of You
from THE PHANTOM OF THE OPERA

Music by ANDREW LLOYD WEBBER
Lyrics by CHARLES HART
Additional Lyrics by RICHARD STILGOE

© Copyright 1986 The Really Useful Group Ltd.
All Rights for the United States and Canada Administered by PolyGram International Publishing, Inc.
International Copyright Secured   All Rights Reserved

Always

Words and Music by
JON BON JOVI

Beautiful in My Eyes

Words and Music by
JOSHUA KADISON

Moderately (not too fast)

You're my peace of mind in this crazy world.
You're ev'ry-thing I've tried to find. Your love is a pearl.

The world will turn and the seasons will change, and all the lessons we will learn will be beautiful and strange.

lines up-on my face from a life-time of smiles, to em-brace when the time comes for one long last while;

Grow Old with Me

Words and Music by
JOHN LENNON

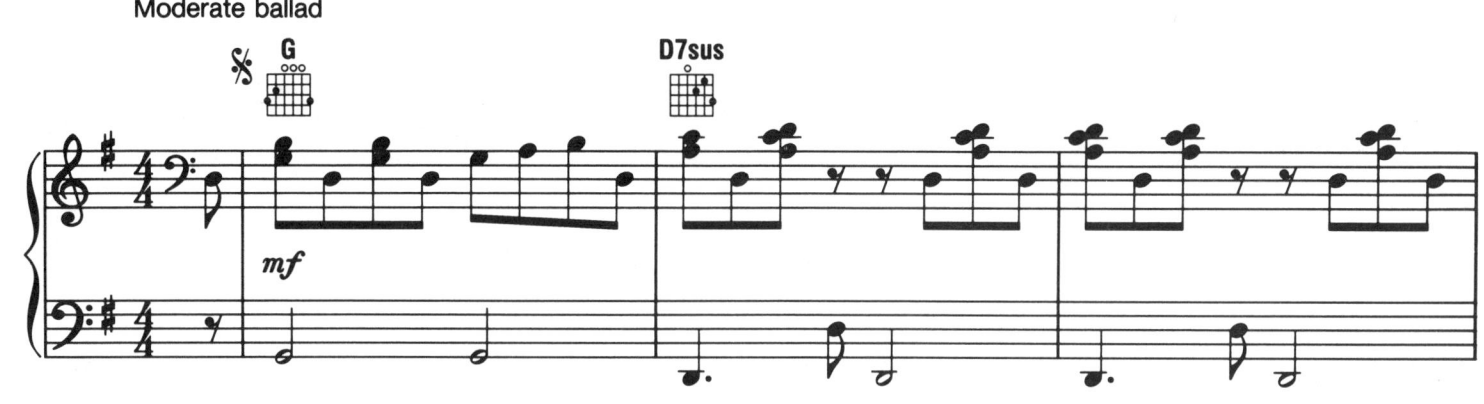
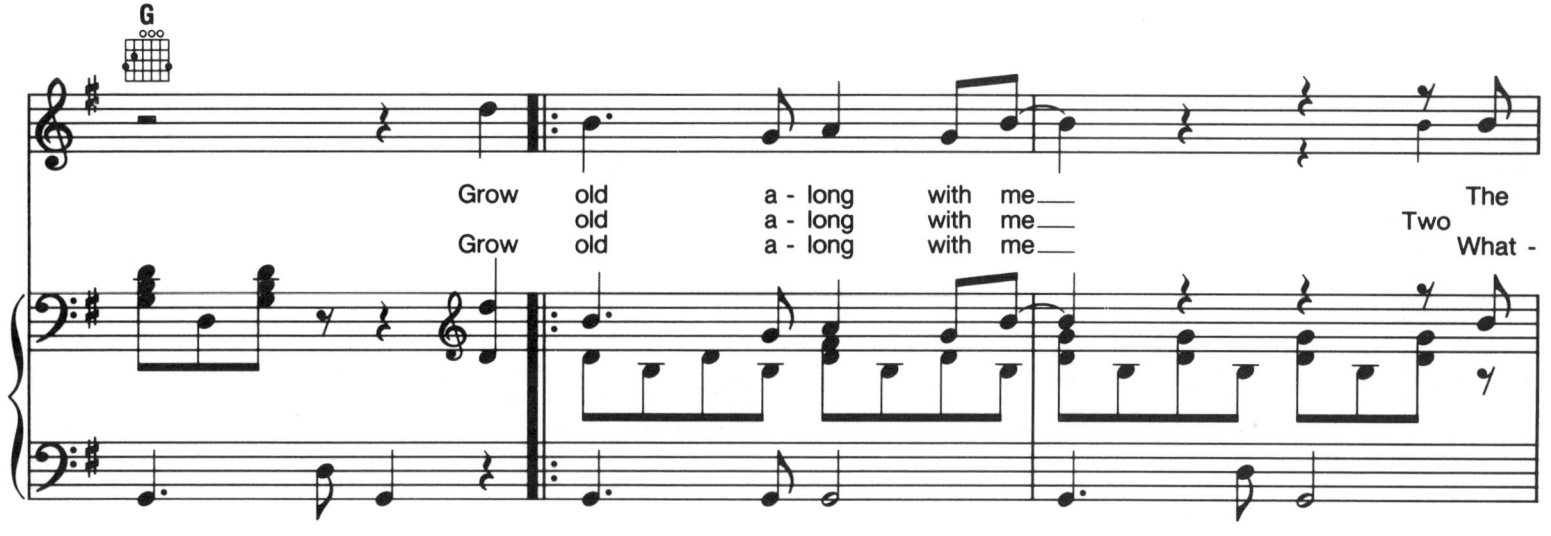
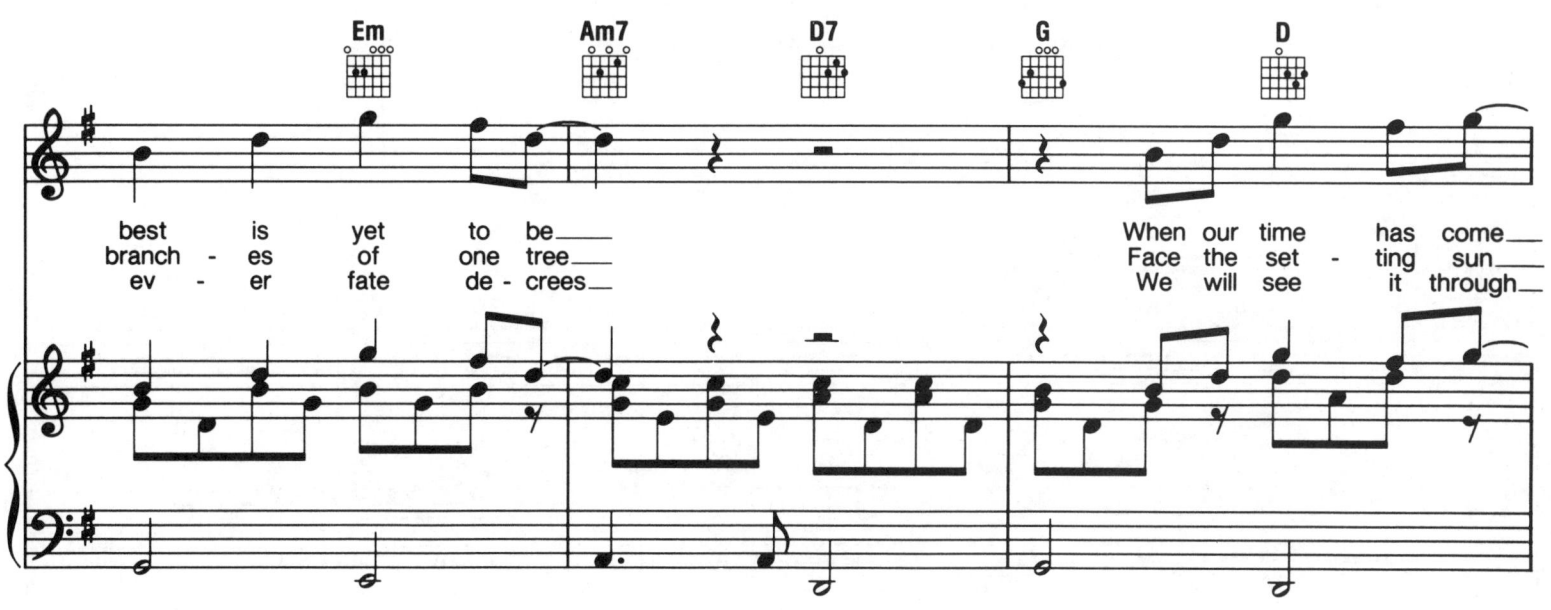

Copyright © 1982 Ono Music
All Rights Administered by Sony/ATV Music Publishing, 8 Music Square West, Nashville, TN 37203
International Copyright Secured   All Rights Reserved

Have I Told You Lately

Words and Music by
VAN MORRISON

I Finally Found Someone

from THE MIRROR HAS TWO FACES

Words and Music by BARBRA STREISAND, MARVIN HAMLISCH,
R.J. LANGE and BRYAN ADAMS

If We Fall in Love Tonight

Words and Music by JAMES HARRIS III
and TERRY LEWIS

Love of a Lifetime

Words and Music by BILL LEVERTY
and CARL SNARE

Save the Best for Last

Words and Music by PHIL GALDSTON,
JON LIND and WENDY WALDMAN

Valentine

Words and Music by JACK KUGELL
and JIM BRICKMAN

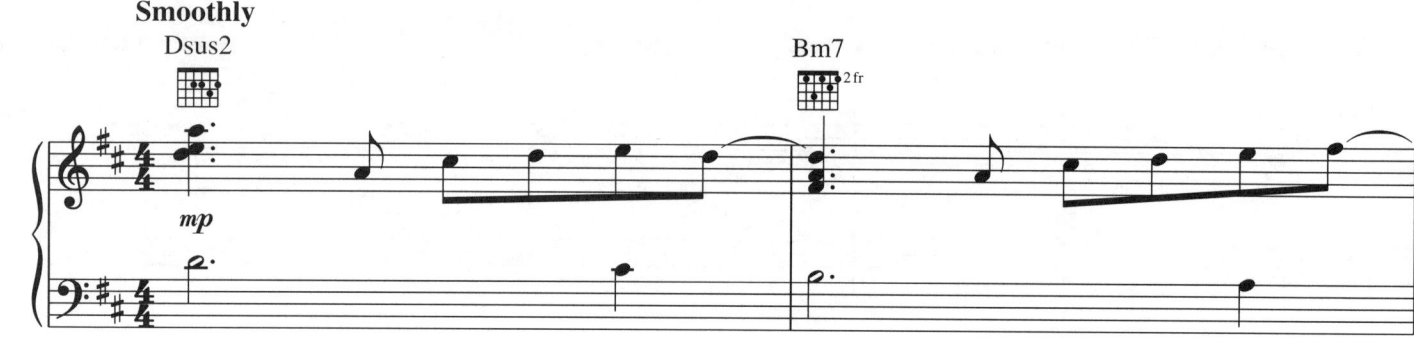
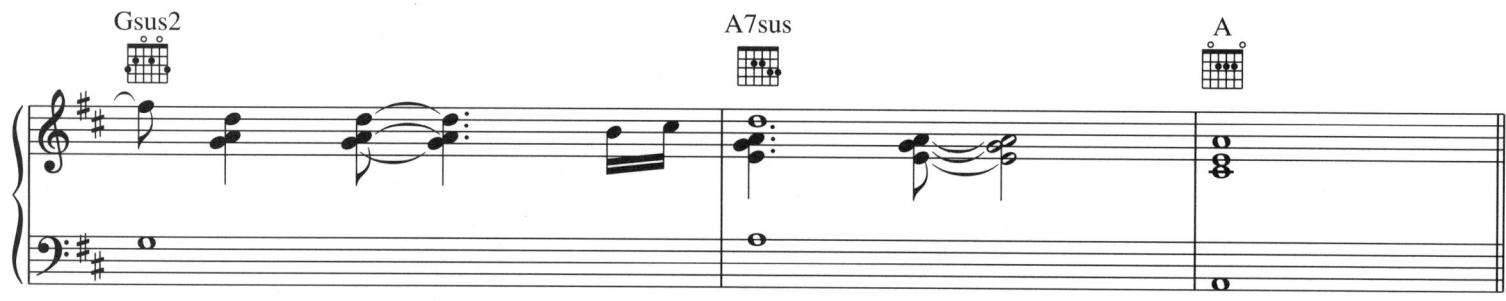

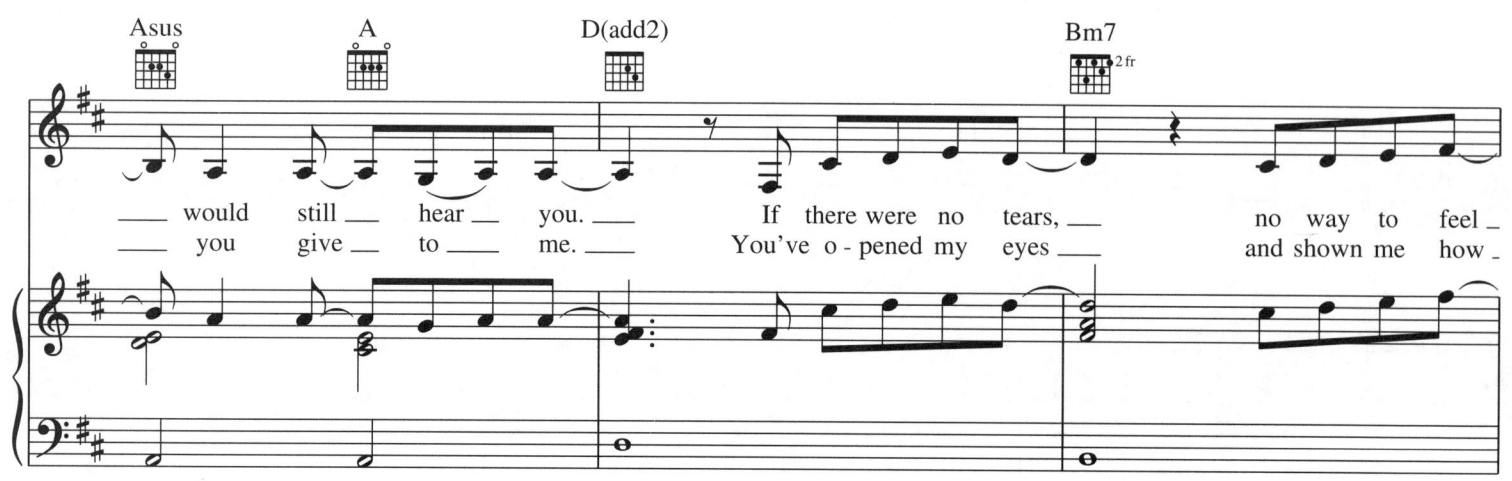

© 1996 EMI APRIL MUSIC INC., DOXIE MUSIC and BRICKMAN ARRANGEMENT
All Rights for DOXIE MUSIC Controlled and Administered by EMI APRIL MUSIC INC.
All Rights Reserved   International Copyright Secured   Used by Permission

The Wedding Song

By KENNY G
and WALTER AFANASIEFF

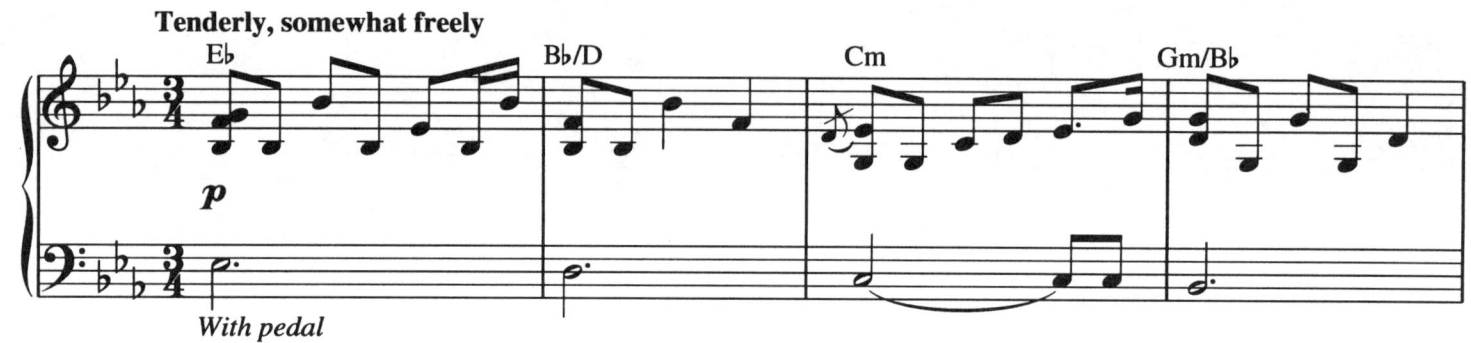

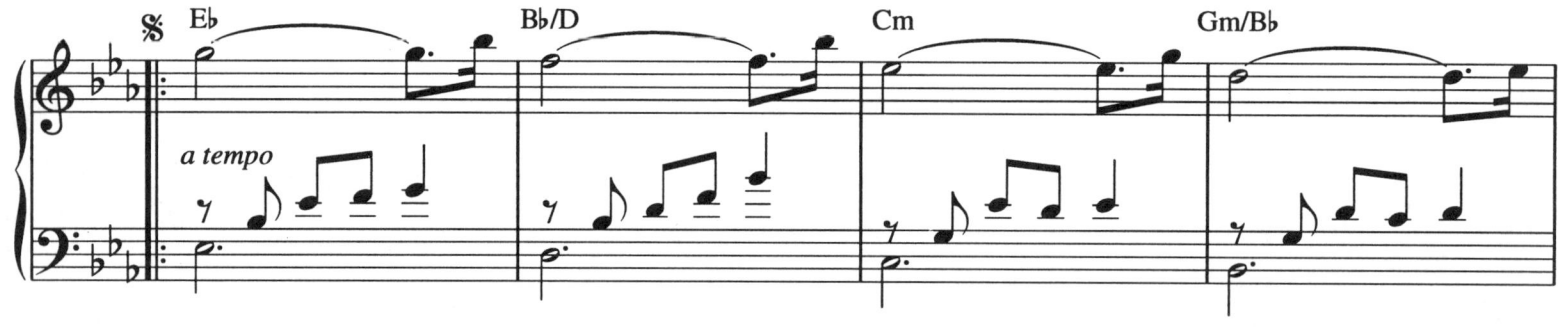

© 1992 EMI BLACKWOOD MUSIC INC., KUZU MUSIC, KENNY G MUSIC, HIGH TECH MUSIC, WB MUSIC CORP. and WALLYWORLD MUSIC
All Rights for KUZU MUSIC Controlled and Administered by EMI BLACKWOOD MUSIC INC.
All Rights for WALLYWORLD MUSIC Administered by WB MUSIC CORP.
All Rights Reserved International Copyright Secured Used by Permission

You and I

Words and Music by
FRANK MYERS

Moderately Slow and Smooth

1. 2. Just you and I, sharing our dreams to-geth-er, and I know in time we'll build the dreams we treas-ure.

3. (See additional lyrics)

© 1982 Colgems-EMI Music Inc.
All Rights Reserved International Copyright Secured Used by Permission

Verse 3:
Just you and I;
We care and trust each other.
With you in my life,
There'll never be another.
We'll be all right,
Just you and I.
(To Chorus:)

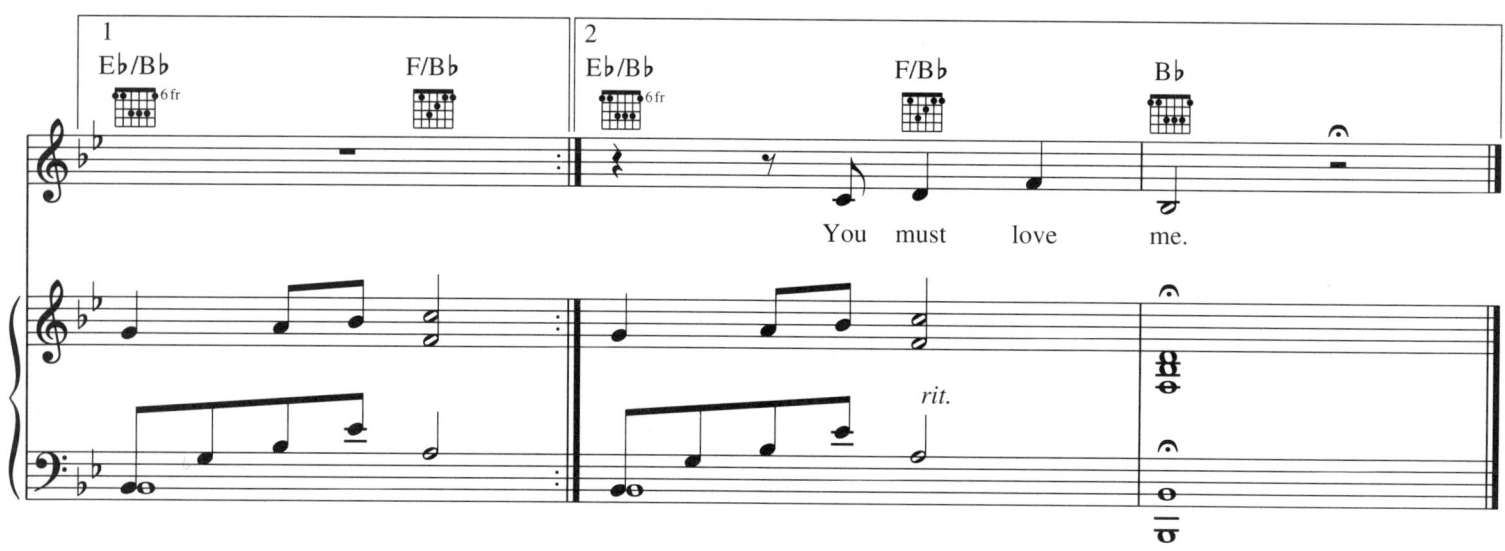

Additional Lyrics

Verse 2: *(Instrumental 8 bars)*
Why are you at my side?
How can I be any use to you now?
Give me a chance and I'll let you see how
Nothing has changed.
Deep in my heart I'm concealing
Things that I'm longing to say,
Scared to confess what I'm feeling
Frightened you'll slip away,
You must love me.